ARROYO CENTER

T0097342

Assessing the Value of Regionally Aligned Forces in Army Security Cooperation

An Overview

Angela O'Mahony, Thomas S. Szayna, Michael J. McNerney, Derek Eaton, Joel Vernetti, Michael Schwille, Stephanie Pezard, Tim Oliver, Paul S. Steinberg

Prepared for the United States Army
Approved for public release; distribution unlimited

For more information on this publication, visit www.rand.org/t/RR1341z1

Library of Congress Cataloging-in-Publication Data is available for this publication.
ISBN: 978-0-8330-9603-6

Published by the RAND Corporation, Santa Monica, Calif.
© Copyright 2017 RAND Corporation
RAND® is a registered trademark.

Support RAND
Make a tax-deductible charitable contribution at
www.rand.org/giving/contribute

www.rand.org

Preface

The Army is in the midst of aligning specific units with geographical regions (regionally aligned forces, or RAF) to strengthen cultural awareness and language skills, facilitate force management, and improve security cooperation (SC) efforts around the world. Given the substantial role that the Army plays in U.S. SC, it is important to understand the RAF's value in making SC more effective.

To address this, the Army asked the RAND Arroyo Center to assess the initial use of a RAF in Africa, focusing on SC, as part of a project titled "Assessing the Value of Regionally Aligned Forces in Army Security Cooperation." This project assessed the RAF's effectiveness in Africa for improving SC planning and execution. This report provides highlights from recent Arroyo Center research on the value of Army RAF to U.S. SC activities, particularly those conducted in Africa.

This research was sponsored by the U.S. Army Deputy Chief of Staff, G-8, and conducted within the RAND Arroyo Center's Strategy, Doctrine, and Resources Program. RAND Arroyo Center, part of the RAND Corporation, is a federally funded research and development center sponsored by the United States Army.

The Project Unique Identification Code (PUIC) for the project that produced this document is HQD136618.

For more information on RAND Arroyo Center, contact the Director of Operations (telephone 310-393-0411, extension 6419; fax 310-451-6952; email Marcy_Agmon@rand.org), or visit Arroyo's website at www.rand.org/ard.

Contents

Figures

CHAPTER ONE

Introduction

Background

With direct military operations in Iraq and Afghanistan reduced, the United States has increased its strategic focus on preparing for future conflict and shaping the international environment to prevent the need for large-scale commitments of U.S. military personnel. In support of this strategy, the Army's regionally aligned force (RAF) concept provides combatant commanders with improved access to forces capable of helping shape the international environment and aligns Army capabilities to an expanded set of joint force requirements (Field, Learmont, and Charland, 2013).

The roots of the RAF concept trace back to an increased emphasis in having U.S. forces work with other militaries, which flows from the 2008 *National Defense Strategy*, in which then–Secretary of Defense Robert Gates stressed the importance of building capacity across a broad range of international partners to strengthen stability globally (U.S. Department of Defense [DoD], 2008). This focus grew in 2010 with the publication of the *National Security Strategy*, which stated that the United States would "continue strengthening its capacity to partner with foreign counterparts, train and assist security forces, and pursue military-to-military [M2M] ties with a broad range of governments" (President of the United States of America, 2010, p. 11). Added impetus for the RAF concept grew from the 2012 defense strategic guidance, *Sustaining U.S. Global Leadership: Priorities for 21st Century Defense*. In that year, the first RAF executive order was published, which aligned Fort Riley's 2nd Brigade Combat Team, 1st Armored Division (2/1 ABCT) to U.S. Africa Command (U.S. AFRICOM) (Headquarters, Department of the Army, 2012b). With that order, Army units began to implement the RAF concept, and U.S. Army Africa (USARAF) staff rapidly employed the newly aligned force to fill planned security cooperation (SC) and operational missions and other emergent requirements.

By proactively engaging the RAF, Army leadership expects that the RAF will help to achieve national and collective objectives across the range of military operations. By enabling greater Army investments in SC, the RAF is expected to reduce future U.S. involvement across the spectrum of conflict—from crisis response, to limited contingency operations, to major operations and campaigns. By increasing Army investments in strategic regional partners and in prevent-and-shape operations, planners assume that the RAF will reduce the likelihood of regional crises and enable partners to face their own security threats more effectively.[1] In those cases in which prevention fails, planners expect that the regional expertise that RAF units will have developed will allow those units to perform better across the range of operations; they will have greater insight into conditions on the ground and experience in conducting operations with foreign partners.

Although the initial intent of the RAF concept was to provide operational forces for combatant commands (CCMDs) to implement SC activities, it has widened to encompass more units, different types of units, and more capabilities. The implementation of the RAF concept continues to evolve as it matures, with its basic components codified in the Army lexicon, doctrine, and planning guidance (Field Manual [FM] 3-22). Although other missions were added to the RAF, SC remains an important mission for CCMDs because it forms a large part of steady-state activities and because the RAF is the force pool from which many of those activities will be sourced. Because the RAF is a major Army initiative and supports high-level policy goals, the Army needs to understand how the concept is being implemented, learn from the implementation process, and adjust course as necessary.

Objectives and Approach

Given this, the Army asked the RAND Arroyo Center to assess the initial use of the RAF in Africa, focusing especially on SC. The initial alignment of the 2/1 ABCT with U.S. AFRICOM has yielded a wealth of experience that could provide useful insights and lessons for future use of the RAF in Africa and elsewhere, enabling greater value and effect from their use. Our assessment spanned the range of planning and execution of RAF missions—from identifying the criteria to assign SC missions to the RAF, to assessing Army force packages and preparations designed to achieve mission objectives, to identifying the capabilities that proved critical to mission success, to learning from deployments as part of the RAF. The overall study goal was to assist the Army, geographic CCMDs, and DoD better align SC missions with national interests and security goals. This study assessed the RAF process, planning, and execution; however, given the short time frames for evaluation and the lack of appropriate data, the study did not assess the effect that the process has had on partner-nation capabilities. But we did develop a planning framework as part of this study that will help prioritize and plan future SC missions, providing a foundation for increasing the effectiveness of SC missions.

---

[1]   Shaping operations are designed to "reassure partners and deter aggression while establishing conditions that support the potential employment of joint forces" (U.S. Army Training and Doctrine Command [TRADOC] Pamphlet 525-3-1, p. 22).

This report provides highlights from recent Arroyo Center research on the value of Army RAF to U.S. SC activities, particularly those conducted in Africa. U.S. SC activities and the alignment of forces may have security implications; as a result, to make this overview as accessible as possible, we have chosen to remove some portions.

Our approach to the research involved a mixed-methods analysis. We examined the policy documents that govern the RAF process and interviewed people from the 2/1 ABCT, USARAF, and experts at U.S. AFRICOM, operational units, and Department of the Army staff. We also treated the experience of the 2/1 ABCT as a case study of RAF efforts. We reviewed previous RAND research on effective planning for SC missions. Informed by these findings, we statistically examined how many USARAF SC activities have been undertaken with politically and militarily compatible partner nations (which we cover in the larger companion document, O'Mahony et al., 2016). For that report, we analyzed 251 USARAF SC activities in Africa in fiscal years (FYs) 2012 and 2013, examining events by their mission type, mission objectives, and partner-nation characteristics. Because the 2/1 ABCT conducted about 16 percent of all USARAF SC activities, limiting our analysis solely to the 2/1 ABCT experience with SC missions would not provide a full picture of USARAF SC activities. This analysis provided the empirical baseline used in the planning framework we developed to help prioritize and plan future SC missions.

CHAPTER TWO

Planning for Security Cooperation Using the Regionally Aligned Force

This chapter reviews the documents that guide SC planning. With that context, we then provide data on the SC activities and force packages that USARAF used in its first year of RAF planning. Third, we summarize what we can learn from recent RAND research on effective planning for SC missions and then what we can learn from the United Kingdom (UK) and France, which have pursued regional alignment for SC and other missions in Africa.

What Guides Security Cooperation Planning?

Multiple documents guide the development of SC activities. The *National Security Strategy*, *National Defense Strategy*, Unified Command Plan (not available to the public), Quadrennial Defense Review, and *National Military Strategy* all call for engagement, deeper cooperation, and building partner capacity (BPC) in general terms.

The Secretary of Defense's strategic planning guidance provides more-specific direction drawn from these strategic documents, tasking CCMDs with developing theater campaign plans for their respective regions to communicate the connection between steady-state activities and strategic end states. The Joint Strategic Capabilities Plan, released by the Chairman of the Joint Chiefs of Staff, complements the Secretary of Defense's strategic planning guidance by translating strategic policy end states into military campaigns and planning guidance for CCMDs (Chairman of the Joint Chiefs of Staff Instruction 3100.01C). Additionally, this plan expands the guidance for SC activities and sets the overall tone for regional engagements.

The theater campaign plan integrates and synchronizes steady-state activities with operational plans, linking the Army service component command (ASCC) and other operational-level commanders to strategic end states and goals. Using this guidance, CCMDs' planners, in coordination with each U.S. embassy country team, develop individual country plans (FM 3-22, p. 1-18). The theater campaign support plan (TCSP) is usually an annex to the theater campaign plan and links Army planning, programming, budgeting, and execution of SC activities (FM 3-22, p. 3-3).

All the documents mentioned above provide the foundational guidance for planning SC activities. In effect, the documents create a road map for planners, starting at the most strategic (and thus general) level of guidance and then focusing on particular aspects of national security and particular regions of the world.

On What Did the Regionally Aligned Force in U.S. Army Africa Focus in Its First Year?

Based on strategic and operational guidance, U.S. AFRICOM's theater strategic objectives (TSOs) focus on several functional areas, which can vary by year, but include such areas as countering violent extremist organizations (VEOs), strengthening maritime security and countering illicit trafficking, strengthening defense capabilities, maintaining strategic posture, and preparing for and responding to crises. In the first functional area, U.S. AFRICOM might identify a VEO of primary concern, as well as other VEOs of concern.

Force Packages That U.S. Army Africa Has Used

In carrying out its SC activities, USARAF has used a range of force packages, from two-soldier traveling contact teams (TCTs) that deploy for a few days, to platoon-sized train-and-equip teams that work with partner forces for several months, to battalion-sized task forces that deploy for a few weeks in support of major exercises, such as Southern Accord 13. TCTs are the most common form of SC force package that USARAF uses. Doctrinally, TCTs are generally two- to three-person DoD teams traveling to the host nation to exchange tactics, techniques, and procedures with the host nation's military to improve understanding, interoperability, and operational capability.

Force Packages That U.S. Army Africa Used in Fiscal Years 2011 Through 2013

In terms of force packages USARAF used in FYs 2011 through 2013, the largest category was M2M contacts, which made up some 64 percent of all USARAF SC events during this period. *M2M contacts* usually refers to TCT and familiarization visits, which are paid for using Traditional Combatant Commander Activities funds (10 U.S.C. § 168). Such activities are military liaison teams, seminars and conferences, exchanges of military and civilian personnel, distribution of publications, and DoD personnel expenses related to the last three activities. M2M Traditional Combatant Commander Activities often encompass such military topics as intelligence, logistics, medicine, professional development, maneuver, military engineering, and combat support. The other categories, in descending order, are State Partnership Program events, which are used to execute M2M-like events, bilateral familiarization and training events, emergency management, environmental remediation exercises, fellowship-style internships, educational exchanges, and civic leader visits; advise-and-assist events, which generally support the Africa Contingency Operations Training and Assistance (ACOTA) program; exercises, which include both the actual training exercises and the planning conferences required to execute them; and train-and-equip events, which include traditional foreign military sales activities and personnel deployed in support of Section 1206, Section 1207, and Trans-Sahara Counterterrorism Partnership programs.[1]

In summary, USARAF conducts an extensive program of SC and uses a wide variety of force packages to carry out these missions. Although the specific number of events held is difficult to establish using the data available to us, the general pattern of many small and short-duration M2M events and fewer larger events is clear across all sources.

What Can We Learn from Recent RAND Research on Building Partner Capacity?

Effective planning is an important ingredient for successfully achieving broader SC objectives oriented toward BPC. Previous RAND research has shown that *BPC efforts are more effective when the United States is consistent in funding and executing BPC activities and includes a sustainment component.* Also, certain partner-nation characteristics make BPC more effective. These include the partner nation's willingness to invest its own resources to support and sustain the capability being sought, having sufficient absorptive capacity to acquire the new capability, high governance indicators, a strong economy, and shared security interests with the United States. Indeed, this last factor, broad interest alignments, is one of the most important predictors of BPC success. BPC thus works best when U.S. planners match BPC activities to U.S. and partner-nation needs and objectives; match BPC activities to the partner nation's absorptive capacity; and undertake institution-building and other efforts that increase the partner nation's absorptive capacity, including building partner-nation sustainment capabilities (Paul et al., 2013, pp. 87–88, 90–91; Kelly, Bensahel, and Oliker, 2011, pp. 106–107; McNerney et al., 2014).

The ability to assess the results of U.S. SC activities is another important component of success. Assessment is important because it informs decisionmaking about the effectiveness of SC activities and enables an adjustment to the existing programs or a recommendation on future SC activities. In addition, assessment can provide important insights into the best means of executing SC activities (Moroney et al., 2011, pp. 1, 3–4). To be effective, however, the assessments need to be guided by specific and measurable objectives with attached indicators and metrics. The assessment process

---

[1]   *Section 1206* and *Section 1207* refer to those sections of the National Defense Authorization Act for Fiscal Year 2006 (Pub. L. 109-163).

also requires trained data collectors and assessors, as well as resources dedicated to the assessment process (Moroney et al., 2011, p. 39).

Successfully executing SC also depends on having carefully selected and properly prepared trainers, advisers, and mentors. The selection of appropriate personnel to be advisers and trainers is important for success because not all soldiers have the requisite personal and behavioral characteristics to conduct such tasks. In particular, such personnel need to be flexible and adaptable. The key to success is prioritizing the selection of experienced and professionally mature personnel with an aptitude for interpersonal communications (Payne and Osburg, 2013, pp. 14–16, 19–21, 32; Kelly, Bensahel, and Oliker, 2011, pp. 82–83).

What Can We Learn from the United Kingdom and France?

The UK has engaged in SC on a global scale but is especially active in Africa and Asia. French engagement has also been global but is concentrated especially in Africa. In both countries, there have been discussions and plans for regional alignment of their forces. Aspects of effective SC practices are evident in the approaches that the two countries follow.

The United Kingdom

Following the UK's 2010 Strategic Defence and Security Review (Cabinet Office and National Security and Intelligence, 2010), and other documents such as the Ministry of Defence's (MOD's) *International Defence Engagement Strategy*, the British Army has begun to align its forces with specific areas of the world. The British Army's approach to international defense engagement has been influenced by other recent strategy documents: the 2011 *Building Stability Overseas Strategy* (Department for International Development, Foreign and Commonwealth Office, and MOD, 2011) and the *International Defence Engagement Strategy*, which MOD published in February 2013 (MOD, 2013). The *International Defence Engagement Strategy* sets out how all defense activity short of combat operations are to be prioritized. It focuses engagement efforts on "those countries which are most important to our national interests, and where we are most likely to achieve the desired effect" (MOD, 2013, p. 3).

The British Army expects its regional alignment and international cooperation to include cooperation with the Royal Air Force and Royal Navy, each of which will be undertaking its own such efforts. UK officials have raised the issue of regional cooperation in the context of larger cooperative efforts with allies, especially with the United States. Both nations agree that this is a core mission that is common to both armies.

Because the areas chosen for regional alignment—for example, North Africa (Maghreb) and the Persian Gulf region—are areas of concern to both countries, UK and U.S. efforts will likely sometimes overlap, which opens up opportunities to develop best practices before attempting to expand cooperation to other allies. There might also be the potential for competition, especially if partnerships are intended to develop better economic links for defense sales.

France

Africa is the major area of French external engagement and forward presence. Thanks to its historical military presence in Africa—or at least Francophone Africa—and its ability to draw personnel from its bases on the continent, the French Ministère de la Défense has succeeded in having expert units and a reliable supply of soldiers for short, training-focused missions for African operations. These two factors, along with limited human and financial resources, have compelled France to embrace, early on, the notion of small, highly flexible, and culturally aware units to perform SC missions on the African continent.

France relies on operational instructional detachments (*détachements d'instruction opérationnelles*, or DIOs) and technical instructional detachments (*détachements d'instruction techniques*, or DITs) to conduct operational cooperation activities. On average, DIOs and DITs, which are teams that deploy to partner nations to provide advice and training, consist of about ten people, but their size can vary according to several factors, including the type of mission, location, and duration, making them highly adaptable force packages.[2] Besides DIOs and DITs, regionally focused national schools (*écoles nationales à vocation régionale*) are another SC tool. Since 1996, France has developed 16 such schools in Africa based on three principles: (1) addressing the specific needs of partner nations, (2) promoting these countries' ownership of professional military education, and (3) promoting regional security (Barbarin, 2012).

Analysis of UK and French SC activities in Africa shows that they spend considerable effort developing regional, national, cultural, and individual understanding of the personalities, cultures, and characteristics of the areas in which they work. In particular, the French subscribe to the notion of small, highly flexible, and culturally aware units to perform SC missions on the African continent. They also emphasize adaptability and synergies among operations, training missions, and permanent bases, although the latter are not necessary. In contrast to the RAF concept, in which U.S. units are not permanently task organized or tailored to support specific CCMDs, both the UK and France have adopted strategies of long-term regional alignment of individual units to specific regions.

---

[2] Email correspondence with former French SC official, April 26, 2014.

CHAPTER THREE

How U.S. Army Africa Planned and Implemented the Regionally Aligned Force Concept

In this chapter, we turn to the question of how USARAF and the 2/1 ABCT implemented the activities selected for SC as part of the RAF concept. Our approach involved two steps. First, we reviewed documents and considered the work completed to date on the RAF concept. We reviewed published opinions, journal and news articles, and relevant policy documents on issues that included force management, national strategy, CCMD guidance, and Army planning processes. The review, combined with the individual experiences of members of the research team, allowed us to gain a general understanding of the problems that RAF implementers face. This information provided a foundation from which to explore how USARAF implemented the RAF concept.

Second, we conducted semistructured interviews with 17 people from the 2/1 ABCT, ten people from USARAF, and other experts at U.S. AFRICOM, within operational units, and from the Department of the Army staff. Interviews elicited first-hand experiences from two separate points of view: Army planners and SC implementers. The interviews advanced our understanding of the RAF concept and the challenges in implementing it.

What Guides U.S. Army Africa Planning for the Regionally Aligned Force Concept?

Theater Army, Corps, and Division Operations, FM 3-94, is the doctrinal guide for USARAF command and staff. It depicts the roles and responsibilities of the ASCC, outlines the request-for-forces process, and establishes mission command relationships. The ASCC has a critical role in the theater campaign planning process, and operational planners are responsible for showing how SC activities support CCMD requirements and plans. Overall, SC operations are a subset of all operations planned and coordinated through the Operations, Maneuver, and Movement Directorate at USARAF headquarters (HQ), but they require a great deal of time and effort to coordinate.

Country and regional plans for SC are created in the plan divisions. Here, USARAF planners must consider many documents and resources, including the U.S.

AFRICOM and USARAF commander's guidance, theater campaign plan, and TCSP. Several other documents guide the development of SC in support of the theater campaign plan, including Army Regulation 11-31, *Army Programs: Army Security Cooperation Policy*; Department of the Army Pamphlet 11-31, *Army Programs: Army Security Cooperation Handbook*; FM 3-22, *Army Support to Security Cooperation*; Army Regulation 12-15, *Security Assistance and International Logistics: Joint Security Cooperation Education and Training*; *Security Cooperation Programs* (Institute of Security Cooperation Studies, 2016), and *The Management of Security Cooperation* (Defense Institute of Security Assistance Management, 2016).

USARAF planners face multiple layers of command guidance, extensive doctrine, sometimes-confusing authorities, and the ever-changing context in which SC activities take place. To help overcome these challenges, planners use the Army methodology framework found in Army Doctrine Publication 5-0 to structure their plans and programs. In theory, planners take the guidance and reference documents and build integrated SC plans for individual countries and regions. These plans are then sorted and prioritized in the USARAF staffing process, which the Security Cooperation Division within the G-3 manages. Here, the SC working group develops recommendations for concept, sourcing, authorities, and funding for SC operations. Multiple authorities, funding streams, programs, and agencies are involved in SC activities.

Once a type of activity has been selected, a funding source needs to be identified. Funding streams are tied to programs and to types of activities, and certain funds can be used only for specific activities. Good knowledge of the complex funding authorities and legal, regulatory, and fiscal constraints is essential. In general, funding for SC is authorized primarily under sections of Title 22 of the U.S. Code, Foreign Relations and Intercourse, for the Department of State and Title 10, Armed Services, for DoD. Title 22 programs include International Military Education and Training, Foreign Military Financing, the Bureau of International Narcotics and Law Enforcement Affairs, ACOTA, Global Peace Operations Initiative, and Partnership for Regional East Africa Counterterrorism. Title 10 programs include Joint Combined Exchange Training; National Guard Bureau State Partnership Program activities; traditional combatant commander activities, such as security-force assistance and foreign internal defense; and combined exercises. Adding to the complexity, more than 30 U.S. government agencies play a role in U.S. engagement with African agencies on the continent, and not all of these activities align neatly in the theater campaign plan.

What Drives U.S. Army Africa Operational Planning for the Regionally Aligned Force Concept?

To direct USARAF in connecting the RAF concept to operational planning, Army HQ staff provides guidance in three basic forms: (1) official direction, (2) leader comments, and (3) informal communication. This is true of most initiatives and appropriate for a concept that, like the RAF, needed to be adaptive in response to changing conditions in the security environment, stakeholder feedback, and lessons from the field.

Official Direction

The Army's December 2012 RAF execution order was the primary source of official direction, providing guidance for USARAF, the 2/1 ABCT, and other Army components on how to prepare for RAF SC and other missions. One way the execution order facilitated adaptability was by establishing nine working groups to continue to address policy, planning, and execution issues as they arose. U.S. Army Forces Command (FORSCOM) uses its annual mission alignment orders to direct alignment of units—from corps to divisions to brigades and enabler units—with CCMDs; it aligned the 2/1 ABCT and U.S. AFRICOM in FY 2013.

During our research, the Army was developing its second modification to the RAF execution order to roll out what it called RAF 2.0. This modification was to emphasize internal and external coordination. Among many other steps, it was meant to institutionalize two organizational constructs that were developed to help translate broad policy guidance into means for executing SC missions. The first—Army Reserve engagement cells and teams—should help coordinate forces drawn from the Army Reserve. The second—institutional support cells—should help coordinate forces drawn from the institutional Army (e.g., HQ staff). Other official direction comes in the form of warning orders, administrative orders, and other messages from Army higher HQ.

Leader Comments

Army leader comments have been another important means of operationally guiding RAF planners. Although Army officials first discussed the RAF concept in 2010 and made public comments about regionally aligning forces in 2011, the concept was kept relatively low key in a public sense until 2012 (Munoz, 2011; see also Lopez, 2012, and McIlvaine, 2012). In October 2012, GEN Raymond T. Odierno stated that the Army would be "aligning unit headquarters and rotational units to Combatant Commands" (Odierno, 2012b). The Army also used journal articles, *Stand-To!* newsletter notices, and even blog posts (Odierno, 2012a; see also Griffin, 2012, and "Today's Focus," 2012). The Army used these communication methods to facilitate a dialogue as the Army refined the concept over time. Like with most new initiatives, senior-leader comments set the broad parameters, while many details about implementation remained to be worked out over time. A January 2013 article by Army officials in the professional military journal *Parameters* attempted to address concerns that had built up about what the RAF was and how the concept would be operationalized (Field, Learmont, and Charland, 2013). The article provided a detailed definition of the RAF and descriptions of their expected mission types and training. Some SC planners have complained about the confusion surrounding the nature of the RAF and the expectations concerning their use. Others, however, noted that a more transparent, if "messy," process for refining the RAF concept has been preferable to a process in which Army higher HQ directed implementation in great detail at the expense of open, constructive debates.[1]

Informal Communication

Whereas official direction has provided planning instructions and leader comments have facilitated discussions, informal communication has driven RAF implementation of SC activities on a day-to-day basis. RAF planners for Africa generally have been satisfied with the process of informal communications among stakeholders, such as U.S. AFRICOM, USARAF, U.S. embassy country teams, and the 2/1 ABCT.[2] According to our interviews, RAF planners for Africa have viewed discussions with units that provide enabling capabilities (e.g., legal, intelligence, medical, logistics) as more effective in some cases than others and at least partially dependent on personal relationships and personalities. For example, USARAF planners established a strong relationship with Combined Arms Support Command at Fort Lee and used informal communication with staff there to organize several deployments of subject-matter experts (SMEs) on SC missions.[3] Planners would typically work out the details of a mission informally by email and phone and then formally submit the requests for forces through official message traffic. These informal communications were central to how planners prioritized missions and identified force packages to support them.

What Are the Strengths and Challenges in Implementing the Regionally Aligned Force Concept?

To assess implementation of the RAF concept, we interviewed Army leaders and planners about the RAF concept and implementation. We asked staff from Army HQ, U.S. AFRICOM, and USARAF to describe the strengths of the RAF concept—how it facilitated SC planning and improved execution of SC missions. We then asked about challenges they faced in implementing the concept. *On the whole, there seemed to be consensus that the RAF concept has been of great value for both planning and executing SC missions. Most concerns focused on how to make a valuable concept even more effective and far-reaching in the future.*

---

[1]   Author interviews with Army planners and leaders, April–September 2014.

[2]   Author interviews with Army planners and leaders, April–September 2014.

[3]   Author interviews with USARAF planners, April 2014.

Regionally Aligned Force Strengths

After the first year of translating RAF guidance into execution, planners identified six strengths.

1. **The RAF were valuable for facilitating deployments of small teams on short notice.** Planners noted that the request-for-forces process for many missions normally requires a 150- to 180-day lead time. The process is generally similar for both large and small deployments, making it frustrating for planners who simply want to deploy a handful of SMEs for several days of consultations with foreign military counterparts. Adaptability is important for managing many small deployments at once across an entire region, such as Africa. Because the 2/1 ABCT was regionally aligned with U.S. AFRICOM, RAF planners could identify and track the availability of required capabilities more easily. By directing stronger cooperation among RAF planners and force providers, RAF guidance also made it easier for USARAF to strengthen its relationships with enabler units. By knowing in advance what capabilities were available, the process for deploying those forces was much simpler and shorter, giving planners some of the adaptability they needed.

2. **The RAF strengthened planning at U.S. AFRICOM's SC workshops.** Before requirements are formally identified, there are many informal discussions and—importantly—planning workshops among stakeholders. These workshops occur at various levels and times, but the most important SC workshop is U.S. AFRICOM's annual Theater Security Cooperation Working Group. DoD and State Department officials, particularly those at the country team level, discuss regional and country objectives and identify potential missions to make progress toward those objectives. As one Army officer noted, "Knowing what we had with the 2/1 [ABCT] helped us to be proactive."[4]

3. **When requirements existed beyond the capabilities of the 2/1 ABCT, its higher HQ—the 1st Infantry Division (ID)—could sometimes fill the need.** This was especially true for capabilities that, like intelligence, surveillance, and reconnaissance, are maintained at the division level.

4. **The 2/1 ABCT and 1st ID were especially helpful in sourcing SC missions that involved tactical and operational training.** The RAF provided for a more reliable pool of U.S. Army trainers for missions (e.g., the ACOTA program) than in the past. Planners have also found it easier to deploy small teams for such programs as the Trans-Sahara Counterterrorism Partnership. The RAF also improved planners' ability to deploy forces for the Joint Chiefs of Staff exercise program, field training exercises, and company-level live-fire exercises. The RAF should also allow for easier sourcing of requirements under the Sec-

---

4 Author interview with USARAF planner, April 2014.

tion 1203 authority Congress granted in FY 2014 to facilitate general-purpose forces training with foreign militaries (Pub. L. 113-66, 2013, § 1203).

5. **USARAF's ability to reach beyond the 2/1 ABCT was valuable for sourcing tabletop exercises and other missions that required more-senior field officers and noncommissioned officers or enabling capabilities, such as military intelligence, logistics, and medical.** Although the process was sometimes challenging, USARAF planners reached out to SMEs from enabler units and personnel from higher HQ, schoolhouses, and other components of the institutional level of the Army. Innovative organizational constructs, such as the Army Reserve engagement cells and institutional support cells, should improve this process further once they are well established.

6. **Combined Joint Task Force—Horn of Africa (CJTF-HOA) found the 2/1 ABCT to be a valuable source of manpower for both SC and security-force missions.** Although the 2/1 ABCT was originally tasked to focus on SC, CJTF-HOA planners requested that a battalion be assigned to the East Africa Response Force mission to provide force protection. While the battalion was serving in this role, CJTF-HOA pieced together SC force packages using a company from that battalion, supplemented by engineering, medical, and logistics elements. The 1st ID provided continuity when one battalion would replace another. Although CJTF-HOA effectively managed these mission assignments, planners were late in initially requesting program funds.

Regionally Aligned Force Challenges

Planners also identified some challenges relating to working through the RAF. Of the challenges identified, there was consensus on eight main points:

1. **RAF planners frequently cited lack of continuity as a potential impediment to improving SC effectiveness.**[5] As the 2/1 ABCT executed its missions over the year, its members' skills reportedly improved in multiple areas, such as program management, deployment planning, stakeholder coordination, situational assessments, cultural awareness, and reporting. Although strong guidance and transition-related workshops play important roles in helping transfer those skills from one unit to the next, many planners that felt the continuity gained by using brigade combat teams (BCTs) from the same division could be even more significant. The 1st ID served a bridging function as one of its BCTs (2/1) transitioned to another (4/1) in June 2014. Several 2/1 ABCT staff previously involved on the ground leading SC missions moved to division HQ at about the time of this transition. Because its personnel directly supported 2/1 ABCT activities and shared knowledge across the division, the 1st ID served

---

5   Author interviews with Army planners and leaders, April–September 2014.

as an institutional repository for RAF experiences in Africa in a way that cannot be replicated externally.

2. **The staff of the U.S. embassy–based offices of SC across much of Africa and the world faced continuity challenges.** These military and civilian personnel have regional and SC expertise and are responsible for managing SC activities at the country level. Although they rotate, their constant engagement with other U.S. embassy staff and with foreign military personnel help them develop deep expertise. Moreover, the offices can create institutional continuity based on smooth transitions and heavy involvement by U.S. Army foreign-area officers who specialize in cultural, regional, and language expertise. Although RAF often benefit from these offices, the offices are almost always quite small and have no formal responsibilities for supporting the RAF.

3. **Although it was clear that the RAF extended beyond the 2/1 ABCT, there was initially confusion about what additional units were included.** Although the RAF concept was a "whole-of-Army" approach, only the 2/1 ABCT understood that it was aligned to U.S. AFRICOM. For all other units, the RAF concept was perceived as unclear. In the case of Africa, only when additional units were explicitly aligned with U.S. AFRICOM did planners perceive that RAF guidance was clear enough to help execute missions that required capabilities that the 2/1 ABCT could not provide.

4. **RAF planners found providing forces for SC activities at the institutional and strategic levels more challenging than at the operational and tactical levels.** The 2/1 ABCT and 1st ID did not have sufficient senior noncommissioned officers and officers to support many strategic engagements, but how RAF guidance helped planners draw on other forces was initially unclear. The RAF concept allowed Army planners to pull forces globally to support missions that 2/1 could not. In reality, tabletop exercises and strategic training events were limited, although planners could fill some gaps with National Guard and other forces. USARAF faced similar challenges supporting an ambitious five-year plan to establish and sustain a logistics school in the Democratic Republic of the Congo. Planners knew that 2/1 would not have sufficient capabilities for much of the requirement, so they worked with Combined Arms Support Command and other organizations to identify additional forces. This complex effort was considered somewhat disjointed, and RAF guidance was not helpful in facilitating it.

5. **Although there was general consensus that military skills are the foundation for effective SC engagements, some RAF planners felt that the cultural knowledge and other skills needed to assist foreign partners effectively were insufficient for some missions.** Planners cited one engagement in the area of human intelligence training that the training team's lack of cultural awareness hampered, despite its members' strong intelligence skills. Other

RAND research indicates that, "to the extent that regional expertise might be required, it will be needed for select positions in headquarters and theater-level enablers" (Markel et al., 2015, p. 28). RAF planners need to consider both U.S. soldiers' subject-matter expertise and their ability to transfer that expertise to foreign forces.[6] The Army and DoD more broadly have several organizations that can help in this area. For example, the Army's 162nd Infantry Brigade's RAF training teams at Fort Polk (replaced by teams from the 3rd Battalion, 353rd Infantry Regiment) provided courses as part of the Joint Readiness Training Center's larger training mission. The Joint Center for International Security Force Assistance and the TRADOC Culture Center (both at Fort Leavenworth) and the Peacekeeping and Stability Operations Institute at the U.S. Army War College provided analytic support and training.

6. **There was limited ability for the 2/1 ABCT or other RAF forces to work effectively with nonstandard weapons, vehicles, and other equipment that some partner military forces used.** Although this concern was relevant in only certain cases, it is an important factor when planning and preparing for particular missions. This is an area in which Army Special Forces and other special operations forces excel. As of the beginning of 2015, there was an effort at Army HQ to address nonstandard equipment training.

7. **Unit commanders in the 2/1 ABCT faced challenges balancing unit readiness against SC.** Some 2/1 forces were unavailable for SC because they had to perform gunnery qualification and other training to keep high readiness levels. These commanders faced a dilemma of being criticized by USARAF leadership if they did not execute SC missions or criticized by Army leadership if readiness declined.

8. **RAF planners identified a need for stronger processes to assess partner security forces, set milestones for progress, and evaluate the effectiveness of missions over time.** These processes were needed both for regionally aligned units and for USARAF and U.S. AFRICOM. For example, RAF planners suggested that TCTs should conduct baseline assessments of partners and not simply "chat about tactics, techniques, and procedures."[7] RAF planners could then use these assessments to develop more in-depth, focused SC activities, which future TCTs could then evaluate, "creating a virtuous cycle rather than constantly reinventing the wheel."[8]

---

[6] For an interesting analysis of cultural knowledge and SC effectiveness, see Taliaferro, Hinkle, and Gallo, 2014.

[7] Author interview with USARAF planners, April 2014.

[8] Author interview with USARAF planners, April 2014.

We understand that U.S. AFRICOM has been strengthening its evaluation processes, USARAF has been working to identify funding for conducting baseline assessments, and—as we discuss later—the 2/1 ABCT developed several assessment tools. But expanding these processes and tailoring them to support RAF activities in particular will require a complex, multiyear effort. U.S. Army Central issued guidance on RAF assessments in August 2014 and has developed a RAF community of purpose to share information on this and other topics (see also Brooks, 2014).

CHAPTER FOUR

How the 2nd Brigade Combat Team, 1st Armored Division, Implemented the Regionally Aligned Force Concept and Lessons Learned

For 15 months between March 15, 2013, and June 15, 2014, the 2/1 ABCT served as a RAF for U.S. AFRICOM. It was initially intended that the 2/1 ABCT would focus solely on conducting theater SC; however, its mission was modified to include "any task suitable to the Combatant Commander."[1] Throughout its time as the RAF for Africa, the 2/1 ABCT conducted SC missions, provided personnel for the East Africa Response Force, which was to be under the operational control of CJTF-HOA, and provided security-force personnel for CJTF-HOA. Most of the 2/1 ABCT's SC engagement with African partner nations was intermittent and involved small teams deployed for relatively short periods of time. It was designated to perform most, if not all, of the train-and-equip activities USARAF envisioned as of July 2013. Field-grade officers tended to bear a heavier burden than most ranks, but even their load was relatively modest. Nevertheless, the 2/1 ABCT was a significant force provider to USARAF's largest exercise, Southern Accord 13, and helped prepare five African partner-nation infantry battalions for deployment in support of collective interests.

The previous chapter examined the planning and implementation of SC missions writ large. This chapter narrows the focus and identifies key lessons from the 2/1 ABCT's experience based on interviews with key personnel.

What Are the Lessons Learned from the Use of the 2nd Brigade Combat Team, 1st Armored Division?

Lessons learned fall into three categories: (1) training and preparation, (2) potential additional training opportunities, and (3) execution.

---

[1] Unpublished Army guidance; authors' interviews with Army planners and leaders, April–September 2014. We conducted semistructured interviews with 17 people from 2/1 ABCT, ten people from USARAF and other experts at U.S. AFRICOM, within operational units, and from the Department of the Army staff. Interviews elicited firsthand experiences from two separate points of view: Army planners and SC implementers. The interviews advanced our understanding of the RAF concept and the challenges in implementing it.

Training and Preparation

The train-up cycle for the 2/1 ABCT blended fulfilling FORSCOM-mandated training requirements with adequate preparation to conduct SC across the African continent. The 2/1 ABCT's methodology for preparing for the RAF mission was first to ensure competency in the decisive-action mission-essential task list (METL), simultaneously training brigade soldiers in core tasks and certifying the brigade to execute its expeditionary-force responsibilities. The validation process culminated in the successful completion of a combat training rotation at the National Training Center in February 2013. Upon completing the rotation, soldiers were considered to be trained in individual and collective METL tasks, allowing them to focus on skills to help them instruct African partner militaries in those same tasks.

After completing the National Training Center rotation, the 2/1 ABCT began to prepare for specific, assigned RAF missions and to complete additional FORSCOM, U.S. AFRICOM, and USARAF requirements. To accomplish this task, the 2/1 ABCT created a brigade-level training capability called Dagger University, which it used to train soldiers preparing to execute SC. Additional requirements imposed on the staff as they created this training capability came from the brigade commander and from individual country requirements.

Those we interviewed valued Dagger University, which focused on culture, regional expertise, and language training. It started as a six-day course, conducted monthly, which intended to provide a basic level of training to soldiers deploying to the U.S. AFRICOM region. It consisted of classroom instruction for one day, with the remainder of the time spent with experts on specific countries and African natives from within the brigade who could offer advice on African culture and languages (Stoutamire, 2013). The course evolved from its inception to include additional training opportunities, exercises, and interactions with the Leader Development and Education for Sustained Peace program from the Naval Postgraduate School, the Asymmetric Warfare Group at TRADOC, the 162nd Infantry Brigade, TRADOC's Culture Center and the center's Cultural Knowledge Consortium, the Peacekeeping and Stability Operations Institute, Joint Improvised Explosive Device Defeat Organization (now Joint Improvised-Threat Defeat Agency), the 10th Special Forces Group, and Kansas State University professors and students.[2]

According to those we interviewed, the Leader Development and Education for Sustained Peace program was one of the most beneficial relationships, providing instruction to leaders and staff officers through a series of seminars over a three-day period to gain an overview of Africa's languages, cultures, economics, governments, and militaries. Each seminar lasted about 90 minutes per topic and included an overview of the issues, as well as country-specific case studies. Personnel attending the seminars were to supplement the information provided with online training modules

---

[2]   Author interviews with 2/1 ABCT personnel, June 18–19, 2014.

and language-training programs. The leaders were to use this information to develop training for their soldiers (Stoutamire, 2013). Additional courses were taught through one-day seminars that focused on individual RAF missions and specific countries.

Other important groups included the 162nd Infantry Brigade, which sent foreign-area officers and personnel from the Asymmetric Warfare Group to Fort Riley to provide additional instruction and share recent experiences in Africa. The 10th Special Forces Group sent personnel to Fort Riley to provide weapon familiarization for the weapon systems that many of the African militaries use, and the Joint Improvised Explosive Device Defeat Organization sent a small team to provide technical and tactical training.

Additional successes came from a partnership with Kansas State University. Soldiers participated in lectures from professors and informal conversations with African students attending the university. According to our interviews, the conversations with the African students were of particular value because they gave direct insight into the daily lives of Africans and helped to set the conditions for the deployment. Conversations typically lasted several hours and were a chance for soldiers to ask questions about the region or country where they were to deploy.

Potential Additional Training Opportunities

The 2/1 ABCT was the pilot organization for the SC-oriented portion of the RAF allocated to USARAF, and, as mentioned above, it had to fulfill training requirements for both FORSCOM and USARAF. Most of these requirements focused on decisive-action METL tasks, with regionally focused training a secondary consideration. Feedback from 2/1 ABCT interviews indicated that additional knowledge and cultural understanding would have been helpful earlier in the training rotation and that more of the training the members received could have contained additional African content.[3]

Building on these findings, we believe that future RAF units would benefit from an earlier start to the regionally aligned portion of their training and should not wait until after a culminating exercise or training-rotation validation to begin culture, regional expertise, and language training. Accordingly, future units should consider the following regionally focused training and education recommendations as those units are aligned under the RAF concept. These recommendations could be enacted without the involvement of FORSCOM or other ASCC mandating these requirements for deployment and could be implemented and managed at the unit level:

- regionally focused medical training
- area-study preparation and assessment training
- increased regionally focused training scenarios and region-specific role-players
- broad-scale regional and cultural awareness training

---

[3] Authors' conversations with 2/1 ABCT personnel, June 18–19, 2014.

- contingency contract, field ordering officer, and pay-agent training (minimum of one per deploying element)
- language training (one key leader per platoon-size element to achieve 0+/0+; competency through a language-training detachment or online program).[4]

With additional coordination or resource allocation, the following training activities could be enacted:

- a country-specific security-force assistance academy based on a CCMD mission set (could leverage the Defense Security Cooperation Agency)
- development of a set of classes or a certification on how to instruct partner nations
- additional CCMD- or ASCC-directed training outside of METL training requested by CCMD
- development of a culture, regional expertise, and language certification process to validate training
- joint personnel-recovery training
- tactical operations center operations training.

Execution

Mission Requirements

Some issues centered around identifying, selecting, funding, and executing missions. For any given SC activity, multiple layers affect the mission. Political, security, and economic dynamics change frequently across Africa, requiring a proactive, adaptive mind-set to accomplish the mission. As conditions changed, USARAF planners had to adjust to accomplish the goals outlined in the theater campaign plan and TCSP, which, in turn, affected the missions and SC activities that the 2/1 ABCT was tasked to fulfill. To address these issues, 2/1 created several support structures and developed processes to increase communication flow with USARAF and with U.S. embassy staff: an armored BCT RAF coordination and execution cell, the position of a 2/1 liaison officer at USARAF, direct coordination with country-desk officers at USARAF, and direct coordination with U.S. embassy country teams.

Coordination issues with U.S. embassy country teams, regional partners, and contractors were particularly important because they reduced the effectiveness of mission-preparation training, delayed mission execution, and increased the overall cost of the mission. Often, changes to the program of instruction or issues with contractors were not realized until 2/1 personnel were on the ground and face to face with the units they were to train. When this happened, overcoming the hurdles and training the unit were up to the unit leader and the soldiers.

---

[4] 0+ listening proficiency is the ability to understand a small number of memorized phrases relevant to the unit's immediate mission. 0+ speaking proficiency is the ability to speak a limited number of memorized and rehearsed phrases relevant to the unit's mission.

During deployments, and then again upon completion of deployment, 2/1 ABCT officers reported successes and failures to the USARAF planners, desk officers, and the 2/1 ABCT RAF coordination and execution cell. Feedback from after-action reports (through the 2/1 ABCT, USARAF, and U.S. embassy staff) helped ensure that proper tracking systems were in place and helped to refine future mission planning and preparation.

Unit Identification

Several officers at the 2/1 ABCT noted that an infantry BCT (IBCT) would have been a more appropriate choice as a RAF for U.S. AFRICOM.[5] Given the infantry-centric nature of African armies, the nature of the conflicts in which the United States' African partners are engaged, and the quick-reaction force requirements of CJTF-HOA, this observation appears valid. Similarly, more–carefully tailored active component and reserve component mobile training teams might be a better way to deliver training to the partner nations.[6] At least two of the 2/1 ABCT's train-and-equip missions appear to have been suboptimally staffed. Although these observations do not call into question the validity of the broader concept of regionally aligning U.S. Army units, they do suggest that, in the future, more consideration should be given to tailoring capabilities aligned with an ASCC.

Adaptability

To successfully complete SC missions, soldiers and leaders from the 2/1 ABCT needed to be adaptable. Once deployed to Africa, the mission criteria, location, or training aids would often change. Many missions had relatively little reach-back capability, as well as limited communications to request clarification or guidance from parent units. Often, young leaders relied on their training and application of the commander's intent to overcome these obstacles. Critical to this was the careful selection of soldiers for the missions, based on personality, level of maturity, ability to communicate, and ability to build relationships. Rank was not as important as these factors.

Course Standardization

As noted earlier, the 2/1 ABCT participated in many small-scale SC training events, five battalion-level training missions, and two large-scale joint training exercises. Each of the battalion-level missions to train partner military units—those of Niger, Guinea, Chad, Uganda, and Malawi—was developed and executed differently from the others. Although the brigade made strides to standardize the coursework and events being trained on these missions, it was only intermittently successful. Some missions were conducted with the brigade in a supporting role and ACOTA trainers taking the lead, while solely brigade personnel conducted other missions. When

---

[5] Author conversations with 2/1 ABCT personnel, June 18, 2014.

[6] Author conversations with 2/1 ABCT personnel, June 18, 2014.

conducting a battalion-level training mission, adoption of a standardized eight-week, 49-person training program should be considered. A more robust trainer team would have the human resources to allow the company to execute multiple training iterations simultaneously, tailor events based on trainer feedback, train battalion staff, conduct after-action reviews, and train to a higher standard because of the better student-to-instructor ratio.

Assessments

Knowing that assessments are an important part of any training cycle, 2/1 developed several tools for use during its SC missions. One of the first developed was an assessment matrix based on the U.S. Army Universal Task List that United Nations (UN) certifying officials used to ascertain the strengths and weaknesses of a trained battalion. This matrix was a crosswalk from Army to UN tasks and displayed the basic tasks that need to be taught to a force for it to be qualified to support UN peacekeeping operations.

Another tool was the "decisive-action big 10"—an assessment and analysis tool used at the National Training Center to measure a unit's progress through a training rotation. The 2/1 ABCT took this tool and adopted it to suit its needs, resulting in the "Big Red One 9." Observer-trainers who accompanied African forces carried this matrix during training and evaluation lanes to guide comments and provide feedback to the rated soldiers.

CHAPTER FIVE

Planning Framework for Assessing Security Cooperation Missions in Different Planning Environments

Chapter Four discussed the 2/1 ABCT mission in some detail and provided some of the key lessons the unit learned from its experience. This chapter turns to a discussion of the planning framework for such missions that we developed to help planners analyze which SC missions might work best, depending on the desired objectives and the characteristics of the partner nation.

What Does the Security Cooperation Planning Process Look Like?

USARAF SC planners navigate a complex process to plan and execute SC missions. Most SC events are the result of both a top-down, goal-oriented planning process and a bottom-up resource planning process, illustrated in Figure 5.1.

Top-down, goal-oriented planning processes begin with national security strategic objectives. CCMDs identify TSOs and identify priority partner nations based on specific guidance from the Secretary of Defense's strategic planning guidance. CCMD SC planners design SC events to accomplish specific military objectives in support of TSOs in priority countries. In contrast, bottom-up resource planning processes focus on funding and personnel availability, supporting State Department and U.S. embassy goals, and providing SC that partner nations request.

SC event planning reflects multiple, often-competing processes. Planners identify a set of SC missions that might meet TSOs most effectively, but, in the end, they plan SC events based on personnel and funding availability and what partner nations want. As our interviews with USARAF and 2/1 ABCT planners highlighted, planners often found it difficult to design effective SC events that matched both top-down and bottom-up planning criteria. For example, planners noted that country teams are not always sure how well their proposed events match up with priority goals. This is even more difficult to identify for an event that has a long lead time. Planners often felt as if they were engaged in a "box-checking exercise" in which they assert that a SC event can contribute to as many TSOs as feasibly apply. As a result, although the match between strategic objectives, partner nations, and SC events is good, like we observed

Figure 5.1
Top-Down Versus Bottom-Up Security Cooperation Planning Process

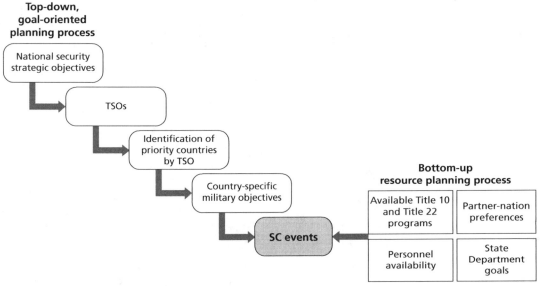

SOURCE: Author analysis.
RAND RR1341/1-5.1

in our statistical analysis (detailed in the larger companion document, O'Mahony et al., 2016), the SC event planning process could be strengthened.

How Can the Security Cooperation Planning Process Be Improved?

To address the difficulty planners identified in matching partner nations to SC activities in support of TSOs, we developed an SC planning prioritization framework to help planners prioritize partner nations for TSOs and to match SC activities to partner-nation characteristics (Figure 5.2). The framework is based on a combination of our review of previous research on SC effectiveness and insights from our analysis of Army SC activities in Africa in 2012 and 2013. Previous research found that tailoring SC to partner nations' characteristics tended to increase SC effectiveness. Our statistical analysis (covered in detail in the larger companion document, O'Mahony et al., 2016) built on these results, finding that partner-nation participation in SC events reflects their political attractiveness to the United States, their military competence, the types of activities that can be conducted, and the geographic combatant commander's strategic objectives. Our framework consists of taking the three categories that we found most important in our statistical analysis of SC event participation and previous research on SC activity type, strategic objectives, and country characteristics and using

Figure 5.2
Security Cooperation Planning Prioritization Framework

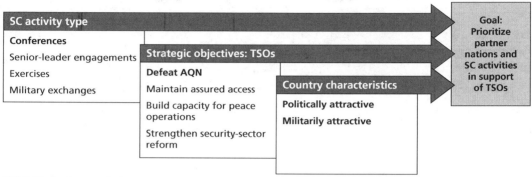

SOURCE: Author analysis.
NOTE: AQN = al Qaeda Network.
RAND RR1341/1-5.2

them as planning tools to understand the relationships and patterns that emerge when we put the data together in different ways.

This framework builds on data already available to SC planners, but it uses the data in a different way. Specifically, SC activities and strategic objectives already get mapped, but mapping is often more of a tracking effort than a planning and assessment effort. Moreover, using our country-characteristic categories and analysis might be especially helpful for CCMD and ASCC planning, in which trade-offs between investing in different SC missions must be made at the regional level.

One of the key observations from our statistical analysis is that, for some strategic objectives (i.e., TSOs), planners' requirements for specific capabilities and specific partner nations constrain those planners. Planners are most constrained when designing SC missions in support of geographically specific strategic objectives (e.g., defeat al Qaeda). In contrast, for other objectives (e.g., strengthen security-sector reform), the range of partner nations and capabilities is much greater. Our framework addresses two questions to assess the constraints under which planners are operating: (1) Are specific partner-nation capabilities required to accomplish the TSO? And (2) Are specific partner nations required to accomplish the TSO? Given these two questions, we developed a matrix with four planning environments:

- environment 1: Specific partner nations and capabilities are required to accomplish the TSO.
- environment 2: Specific partner nations are required to accomplish the TSO.
- environment 3: Specific partner capabilities are required to accomplish the TSO.
- environment 4: Neither specific partner nations nor capabilities are required to accomplish the TSO.

For environments 2 and 3, SC planners need to identify optimal mixes of countries and SC activities to accomplish CCMD TSOs. Using the framework, planners can identify what types of activities and mission objectives were most common as partner nations' political and military attractiveness varied. This type of information highlights how planners can target different activities to different types of countries and how different types of countries might be effective partners in support of different types of TSOs. Overall, as countries' political and military attractiveness increase, the number and quality of SC engagements also increase. For countries characterized by low political and military attractiveness, SC engagements are typified by conferences and multilateral exercises. In contrast, for countries characterized by high political and military attractiveness, M2M engagements that increase information-sharing and interoperability provide greater leverage for accomplishing TSOs.

CHAPTER SIX

Findings and Recommendations

As the Army prepares for a complex future operating environment, the RAF concept plays a critical role positioning the Army as a globally responsive, regionally engaged force (U.S. Army, 2014). The 2014 *Army Strategic Planning Guidance* states (U.S. Army, 2014, p. 14),

> The goal of regional alignment is to provide combatant commanders predictable, task-organized, and responsive capabilities . . . across the full range of military operations, to include joint task force–capable headquarters, crisis or contingency response, operations support, theater security cooperation, and bilateral or multilateral military exercises . . . . Regional alignment also prepares Army forces to build sustainable capacity in partners and allies to address common security challenges.

Informed by our interviews and our analysis of the data, *our overall assessment is that the RAF concept can help the Army to more effectively undertake its SC missions.* The alignment of the 2/1 ABCT to U.S. AFRICOM improved the efficiency of SC planning and preparation. The success of the RAF concept as a process more broadly will depend on structured planning, agility, and access to appropriate personnel. The RAF's ability to carry out SC missions successfully will depend on planners' abilities to match SC activities to TSOs and partner-nation conditions.

Findings

Regionally Aligned Force Implementation, Planning, and Training Processes

We focused our empirical analysis of the RAF concept on the 2/1 ABCT's experiences as a regionally aligned BCT for U.S. AFRICOM. Providing personnel for RAF purposes was not the brigade's sole mission. RAF activities occur alongside other missions that BCTs undertake. As part of its RAF mission, the 2/1 ABCT provided two battalion task forces to provide security for CJTF-HOA, and they formed the bulk of the newly established East Africa Response Force. The East Africa Response Force executed noncombatant-evacuation operations in South Sudan and contributed to other operational missions in the region.

The 2/1 ABCT accomplished a considerable number of SC activities. It deployed 655 soldiers from every battalion in the brigade to more than 26 countries, participated in two separate exercises, and trained five partner-nation infantry battalions and one military police company. While acting as the RAF, the brigade provided personnel for approximately 16 percent of USARAF-directed SC activities.

The two largest personnel commitments the brigade made in support of its RAF mission were operational support to CJTF-HOA and to the Southern Accord exercise. The largest personnel strain the RAF mission placed on 2/1 was on field-grade officers (O-4, O-5, and O-6), on whom the Army often called to deploy as part of two-person TCTs.

A key challenge we identified in our interviews with 2/1 and USARAF planners is the uncertainty and complexity involved in planning and training for missions that span an entire continent. The 2/1 ABCT worked with Kansas State University to design a short training program to help its soldiers develop regional knowledge and set up a RAF operations cell, planning cell, and lessons-learned cell to assist with mission planning. The 2/1 ABCT developed these programs over time to address the complexity and uncertainty it encountered. More can still be done to structure the RAF planning process. We found that building greater planning time and developing a structured planning process for RAF missions in Africa might improve mission effectiveness. For example, we found that, although CJTF-HOA effectively managed its mission assignments, planners were initially late in requesting program funds.

The RAF concept reaches beyond the BCTs assigned to each region. For example, during the period we examined, most SC M2M engagements in U.S. AFRICOM were not staffed from the 2/1 ABCT. Because senior DoD leaders support a greater focus on building the capacity of foreign security sectors at the institutional and strategic levels, the implementation of the RAF concept beyond BCTs will be particularly important.

One of the key benefits of the RAF concept is that it ensures a predictable source of personnel to meet USARAF needs. RAF units must prepare to take on the full range of military operations. It is important for these units to understand how to execute SC and force protection, offensive operations, and other tasks. Critical to effectively balancing these opposing tasks is establishing the correct level and type of training RAF units receive. Successful completion of direct-action METL tasks is critical to the ability of U.S. soldiers to effectively train partner-nation forces. Also, we found that RAF units experienced difficulty delivering training to partner-nation units with nonstandard equipment, so it will be important for Army HQ to continue its efforts to improve the ability of general-purpose forces to conduct security-force assistance through nonstandard equipment training.

Regional Alignment for Security Cooperation

Success in SC missions depends on matching SC activities to TSOs and partner-nation conditions—specifically, what we refer to as partner nations' political and military compatibility. It is crucial for RAF planners to determine whether advancing a TSO requires building a particular partner capability and whether it requires working with a particular partner nation. Regional alignment is expected to increase the regional expertise that RAF units develop, foster greater insight into conditions on the ground, and experience conducting operations with foreign partners. This will enable planners to match SC activities to partner-nation capabilities and preferences. Moreover, regional alignment might intensify Army engagement activities, creating new collaboration opportunities that Army planners have not yet fully explored.

Planners face a variety of constraints. For some strategic objectives, requirements for specific capabilities or specific partner nations constrain planners. Planners are most constrained when designing SC missions in support of geographically specific strategic objectives (e.g., defeat al Qaeda). In contrast, for other objectives (e.g., strengthen security-sector reform), the range of partner nations and capabilities is much greater. Tailoring SC to partner nations' characteristics tends to increase SC effectiveness. Planners need to assess the available mix of partner nations and activities.

We found that, on average, USARAF SC events were most likely to include partner nations that were most politically and militarily attractive. This was particularly the case for intelligence engagements, in which events included countries that were politically most reliable for the United States and militarily most capable. In contrast, for SC events focused on particular strategic objectives, such as counterterrorism, geographic conditions, rather than country compatibility, played a key role in partner selection. For countries that were less politically or militarily attractive, USARAF SC planners limited SC events to such activities as conferences, exercises, medical engagements, and senior-leader engagements. These types of activities provided the basis for early relationship-building and for operations deconfliction. For countries with greater political or military compatibility, USARAF planners emphasized M2M engagements that could build interoperability.

Our empirical assessment of USARAF SC events found that planners did a good job working within their constraints to match SC activities to TSOs and partner-nation conditions. However, the SC event planning process could be strengthened. Our interviews suggested that some activities remain planned in an ad hoc or reactive manner. We developed an SC planning framework to help SC planners identify optimal mixes of countries and SC activities to accomplish CCMD TSOs.

Recommendations

According to our research, the RAF concept, as it was applied to Africa, has had considerable benefits in terms of its flexibility and agility in responding to the evolving security environment. That said, we have identified some areas in which the RAF concept can improve as it evolves—for the Army and for RAF planners.

For the Army

- **Increase the use of senior-leader public comments and informal communication to improve understanding of how to translate formal RAF guidance into execution.** Soldiers and other stakeholders continue to express confusion about the RAF, yet the RAF must continue to grow and evolve to be effective on a global scale. A multipronged communication approach will allow for the greatest agility in responding to changing conditions in the security environment, stakeholder feedback, and lessons from the field.
- **Consider selecting one division to align permanently with each CCMD.** This would enable greater long-term institutional expertise and relationship-building for each region.
- Given the infantry-centric nature of African armies, the nature of the conflicts in which the United States' African partners are engaged, and CJTF-HOA's quick-reaction force requirements, **consider assigning an IBCT (instead of an armored BCT) for the RAF in Africa**. An IBCT might represent the best match between the types of SC missions that are appropriate for accomplishing U.S. national security objectives with African partner nations and the specialties available within the assigned RAF, and it could result in the least-adverse effects on the assigned brigade's overall readiness.
- Because DoD leaders support a greater focus on BPC at the institutional level, **add greater specificity and concrete examples to RAF guidance to help planners reach more effectively into the institutional Army and elsewhere to find potential sources of personnel**. RAF 2.0 constructs, such as the Army Reserve engagement cells and institutional support cells discussed above, are examples of how this can be done.
- **Identify, publicize, maintain, and catalog potential opportunities for RAF units to obtain support inside and outside the government and to help them understand and make greater use of their options for developing cultural awareness, knowledge transfer, and other training skills.** The relationship between the 2/1 ABCT and Dagger University is a good example.
- **Conduct a more thorough review of readiness requirements in the context of the RAF, followed by clear guidance to help manage the balance between maintaining high unit readiness and conducting SC missions.**

- **Facilitate an annual RAF assessment workshop to share best practices among all ASCCs.** As discussed above, confusion remains about how to implement the RAF. As the concept is applied globally, it will be especially important for Army and other stakeholders to engage in wide-ranging discussions about what is working and where problems remain. Discussions about the utility of analytic tools, such as the planning framework we provide above, could be a part of these events.
- **Have BCTs go through a validation exercise before deploying on an SC mission.** As we saw in our analysis of the 2/1 ABCT, learning in the field can be applied back to future training. A validation exercise that tests how much units have absorbed new and evolving lessons could improve agility.
- Because no single brigade contains sufficient subject-matter expertise to cover all SC missions and because drawing expertise from elsewhere can be challenging, **consider developing simpler and clearer methods to support RAF brigades with the right SMEs from across the Total Army and beyond**.

For Regionally Aligned Force Planners
- **Use our planning framework to help match SC activities to TSOs and partner-nation conditions.**
- **Collaborate with special operations forces to institutionalize how forces aligned within each geographic CCMD identify, plan, and prepare for missions involving nonstandard equipment.** As we discussed above, there are times when expertise with nonstandard equipment would be valuable for RAF units, and previous RAND work (Rohn et al., 2014) has shown the value of the RAF engaging U.S. special operators to gain this expertise and for other purposes.
- As discussed above, the regionally focused portion of RAF unit training should be started earlier than was the case for the 2/1 ABCT. This argues for **slightly amending FORSCOM guidance to ensure that future units consider regionally focused training and its relevance to SC early in their training**:
  - regionally focused medical training
  - area-study preparation and assessment training
  - increased regionally focused training scenarios and region-specific role-players
  - broad-scale regional and cultural awareness training
  - contingency contract, field ordering officer, and pay-agent training (minimum of one per deploying element)
  - language training (one key leader per platoon-size element to achieve 0+/0+; competency through a language-training detachment or online program).

The RAF concept has made the process of allocating and delivering U.S. SC in U.S. AFRICOM easier. In the spirit of continuous improvement, a great deal more can be done, especially in terms of better understanding the effectiveness of SC. But the fact that more needs to be done should in no way detract from the overall improvement of U.S. SC that the RAF concept has already achieved.

Acknowledgments

We are grateful to the Army Deputy Chief of Staff, G-8, for sponsoring the study. We thank Timothy Muchmore, Headquarters, Department of the Army, G-8, for monitoring the study and providing constructive feedback during its course.

We also thank the following people from U.S. Army Africa Headquarters: COL Pedro G. Almeida, Perry L. Buxo, David L. Spencer, LTC Brad A. Bane, Jim Matisse, LTC David Howe, LTC Robert Garbarino, LTC Gerry Dolan, Jim Metzger, Matthew Koehler, and Jimmy Grizzard.

At Headquarters, Department of the Army, Operations Directorate, we thank COL Jason A. Charland, LTC Gary Casey, MAJ David Kogon, and Robert Maginnis.

We are grateful to the soldiers of the 2nd Brigade Combat Team, 1st Armored Division, at Fort Riley, Kansas, who shared their insights and experiences with us. The following were especially helpful: LTC Charles Slagle, MAJ Kevin Bukowski, and William Simmons. We also thank Steven Graham of Kansas State University.

Lisa Turner put the report into RAND style and format.

Abbreviations

2/1 ABCT	2nd Brigade Combat Team, 1st Armored Division
ACOTA	Africa Contingency Operations Training and Assistance
ASCC	Army service component command
BCT	brigade combat team
BPC	building partner capacity
CCMD	combatant command
CJTF-HOA	Combined Joint Task Force—Horn of Africa
DIO	*détachement d'instruction opérationnelle*, or operational instructional detachment
DIT	*détachement d'instruction technique*, or technical instructional detachment
DoD	U.S. Department of Defense
FM	field manual
FORSCOM	U.S. Army Forces Command
FY	fiscal year
HQ	headquarters
IBCT	infantry brigade combat team
ID	infantry division
M2M	military to military
METL	mission-essential task list
MOD	United Kingdom Ministry of Defence

RAF	regionally aligned force
SC	security cooperation
SME	subject-matter expert
TCSP	theater campaign support plan
TCT	traveling contact team
TRADOC	U.S. Army Training and Doctrine Command
TSO	theater strategic objective
UK	United Kingdom
UN	United Nations
U.S. AFRICOM	U.S. Africa Command
USARAF	U.S. Army Africa
VEO	violent extremist organization

References

Army Doctrine Publication 5-0—*See* Headquarters, Department of the Army, 2012a.

Army Regulation 11-31—*See* Headquarters, Department of the Army, 2013b.

Army Regulation 12-15—*See* Headquarters, Department of the Army, 2011.

Barbarin, Tugdual, "Les Écoles Nationales à Vocation Régionale, un outil novateur pour l'instauration d'une sécurité nationale et régionale," Institut de Recherche Stratégique de L'École Militaire, Ministère de la Défense, September 10, 2012. As of June 8, 2015:
http://www.defense.gouv.fr/irsem/publications/lettre-de-l-irsem/les-lettres-de-l-irsem-2012-2013/
2012-lettre-de-l-irsem/lettre-de-l-irsem-n-7-2012/dossier-strategique/les-ecoles-nationales-a-vocation-
regionale-un-outil-novateur-pour-l-instauration-d-une-securite-nationale-et-regionale

Brooks, Rosa, "Portrait of the Army as a Work in Progress," *Foreign Policy*, May 8, 2014. As of June 9, 2015:
http://foreignpolicy.com/2014/05/08/portrait-of-the-army-as-a-work-in-progress/

Cabinet Office and National Security and Intelligence, *The Strategic Defence and Security Review: Securing Britain in an Age of Uncertainty*, October 19, 2010. As of July 25, 2016:
https://www.gov.uk/government/publications/
the-strategic-defence-and-security-review-securing-britain-in-an-age-of-uncertainty

Chairman of the Joint Chiefs of Staff, *Joint Strategic Planning System*, Chairman of the Joint Chiefs of Staff Instruction 3100.01C, November 20, 2015. As of August 13, 2016:
http://dtic.mil/cjcs_directives/cdata/unlimit/3100_01a.pdf

Chairman of the Joint Chiefs of Staff Instruction 3100.01C—*See* Chairman of the Joint Chiefs of Staff, 2015.

Defense Institute of Security Assistance Management, *The Management of Security Cooperation*, edition 35.0, Wright-Patterson Air Force Base, Ohio, March 2016. As of July 25, 2016:
http://www.iscs.dsca.mil/_pages/resources/default.aspx?section=publications&type=greenbook

Department for International Development, Foreign and Commonwealth Office, and Ministry of Defence, *Building Stability Overseas Strategy*, London, July 1, 2011. As of July 20, 2016:
https://www.gov.uk/government/publications/building-stability-overseas-strategy

Department for International Development, Foreign and Commonwealth Office, and MOD—*See* Department for International Development, Foreign and Commonwealth Office, and Ministry of Defence.

Department of the Army Pamphlet 11-31—*See* Headquarters, Department of the Army, 2015.

Field, Kimberly, James Learmont, and Jason Charland, "Regionally Aligned Forces: Business *Not* as Usual," *Parameters*, Vol. 43, No. 3, January 2013, pp. 55–63. As of July 20, 2016:
http://oai.dtic.mil/oai/oai?verb=getRecord&metadataPrefix=html&identifier=ADA598574

FM 3-22—*See* Headquarters, Department of the Army, 2013a.

FM 3-94—*See* Headquarters, Department of the Army, 2014.

Griffin, Steve, "Regionally-Aligned Brigades: There's More to This Plan Than Meets the Eye," *Small Wars Journal*, September 19, 2012. As of July 20, 2016:
http://smallwarsjournal.com/printpdf/13237

Headquarters, Department of the Army, *Security Assistance and International Logistics: Joint Security Cooperation Education and Training*, Army Regulation 12-15, Secretary of the Navy Instruction 4950.4B, Air Force Instruction 16-105, January 3, 2011. As of August 13, 2016:
http://www.disam.dsca.mil/itm/JSCET/JSCET%203%20Jan%2011%20R12_15.pdf

———, *The Operations Process*, Army Doctrine Publication 5-0, May 2012a.

———, *Regionally Aligned Forces (RAF) Execute Order (EXORD)*, December 22, 2012b, not available to the general public.

———, *Army Support to Security Cooperation*, Washington, D.C., Field Manual 3-22, January 22, 2013a.

———, *Army Programs: Army Security Cooperation Policy*, Army Regulation 11-31, March 21, 2013b.

———, *Theater Army, Corps, and Division Operations*, Field Manual 3-94, April 21, 2014.

———, *Army Programs: Army Security Cooperation Handbook*, Department of the Army Pamphlet 11-31, February 6, 2015.

Institute of Security Cooperation Studies, *Security Cooperation Programs, Fiscal Year 2016*, revision 16.2, c. 2016. As of July 25, 2016:
http://www.iscs.dsca.mil/documents/pubs/security_cooperation_programs_16_2.pdf

Kelly, Terrence K., Nora Bensahel, and Olga Oliker, *Security Force Assistance in Afghanistan: Identifying Lessons for Future Efforts*, Santa Monica, Calif.: RAND Corporation, MG-1066-A, 2011. As of July 20, 2016:
http://www.rand.org/pubs/monographs/MG1066.html

Lopez, C. Todd, "Army Will Prepare for Future with Regionally Aligned Forces," U.S. Army, October 23, 2012. As of June 9, 2015:
http://www.army.mil/article/89819/Army_will_prepare_for_future_with_regionally_aligned_forces/

Markel, M. Wade, Bryan W. Hallmark, Peter Schirmer, Louay Constant, Jaime Hastings, Henry A. Leonard, Kristin J. Leuschner, Lauren A. Mayer, Caolionn O'Connell, Christina Panis, Jose Rodriguez, Lisa Saum-Manning, and Jonathan Welch, *A Preliminary Assessment of the Regionally Aligned Forces (RAF) Concept's Implications for Army Personnel Management*, Santa Monica, Calif.: RAND Corporation, RR-1065-A, 2015. As of July 20, 2016:
http://www.rand.org/pubs/research_reports/RR1065.html

McIlvaine, Rob, "Odierno: Regional Alignments to Begin Next Year," U.S. Army, May 16, 2012. As of June 9, 2015:
http://www.army.mil/article/79919/

McNerney, Michael J., Angela O'Mahony, Thomas S. Szayna, Derek Eaton, Caroline Baxter, Colin P. Clarke, Emma Cutrufello, Michael McGee, Heather Peterson, Leslie Adrienne Payne, and Calin Trenkov-Wermuth, *Assessing Security Cooperation as a Preventive Tool*, Santa Monica, Calif.: RAND Corporation, RR-350-A, 2014. As of July 20, 2016:
http://www.rand.org/pubs/research_reports/RR350.html

Ministry of Defence, *International Defence Engagement Strategy*, London, February 6, 2013. As of July 20, 2016:
https://www.gov.uk/government/publications/international-defence-engagement-strategy

MOD—*See* Ministry of Defence.

Moroney, Jennifer D. P., Beth Grill, Joe Hogler, Lianne Kennedy-Boudali, and Christopher Paul, *How Successful Are U.S. Efforts to Build Capacity in Developing Countries? A Framework to Assess the Global Train and Equip "1206" Program*, Santa Monica, Calif.: RAND Corporation, TR-1121-OSD, 2011. As of July 20, 2016:
http://www.rand.org/pubs/technical_reports/TR1121.html

Munoz, Carlo, "New Army Units to Tackle Military Co-Op Missions," *Breaking Defense*, October 11, 2011. As of June 9, 2015:
http://breakingdefense.com/2011/10/new-army-units-to-tackle-military-co-op-missions/

Odierno, Raymond T., "Regionally Aligned Forces: A New Model for Building Partnerships," *Army Live*, March 22, 2012a. As of June 9, 2015:
http://armylive.dodlive.mil/index.php/2012/03/aligned-forces/

———, "CSA Remarks at AUSA Eisenhower Luncheon (as Delivered)," U.S. Army, October 23, 2012b. As of June 9, 2015:
http://www.army.mil/article/89823/
October_23__2012____CSA_Remarks_at_AUSA_Eisenhower_Luncheon__As_Delivered_/

O'Mahony, Angela, Thomas S. Szayna, Michael J. McNerney, Derek Eaton, Joel Vernetti, Michael Schwille, Stephanie Pezard, Tim Oliver, and Jerry M. Sollinger, *Assessing the Value of Regionally Aligned Forces in Army Security Cooperation*, Santa Monica, Calif.: RAND Corporation, 2016, not available to the general public.

Paul, Christopher, Colin P. Clarke, Beth Grill, Stephanie Young, Jennifer D. P. Moroney, Joe Hogler, and Christine Leah, *What Works Best When Building Partner Capacity and Under What Circumstances?* Santa Monica, Calif.: RAND Corporation, MG-1253/1-OSD, 2013. As of July 20, 2016:
http://www.rand.org/pubs/monographs/MG1253z1.html

Payne, Leslie Adrienne, and Jan Osburg, *Leveraging Observations of Security Force Assistance in Afghanistan for Global Operations*, Santa Monica, Calif.: RAND Corporation, RR-416-A, 2013. As of July 21, 2016:
http://www.rand.org/pubs/research_reports/RR416.html

President of the United States of America, *National Security Strategy*, Washington, D.C.: White House, May 2010. As of November 25, 2014:
http://www.whitehouse.gov/sites/default/files/rss_viewer/national_security_strategy.pdf

Public Law 109-163, National Defense Authorization Act for Fiscal Year 2006, January 6, 2006. As of July 25, 2016:
https://www.gpo.gov/fdsys/pkg/STATUTE-119/pdf/STATUTE-119-Pg3136.pdf

Public Law 113-66, National Defense Authorization Act for Fiscal Year 2014, December 26, 2013. As of July 21, 2016:
https://www.gpo.gov/fdsys/pkg/PLAW-113publ66/pdf/PLAW-113publ66.pdf

Rohn, Laurinda L., Henry A. Leonard, Stephen Watts, Molly Dunigan, and Linda Robinson, *Interdependence Between Army Special Operations and Conventional Forces: Options for Improvement and the Army's Regionally Aligned Forces Concept*, Santa Monica, Calif.: RAND Corporation, June 2014, not available to the general public.

Stoutamire, Daniel, "'Daggers' Get Insight on Culture for New Mission," Fort Riley, Kan., April 9, 2013. As of June 5, 2015:
http://www.riley.army.mil/News/ArticleDisplay/tabid/98/Article/471966/
daggers-get-insight-on-culture-for-new-mission.aspx

Taliaferro, Aaron, Wade P. Hinkle, and Alexander O. Gallo, "Foreign Culture and Its Effect on US Department of Defense Efforts to Train and Advise Foreign Security Forces," *Small Wars Journal*, November 26, 2014. As of June 9, 2015:
http://smallwarsjournal.com/jrnl/art/
foreign-culture-and-its-effect-on-us-department-of-defense-efforts-to-train-and-advise-fore

"Today's Focus: Regionally Aligned Forces," *Stand-To!* December 20, 2012.

U.S. Army, *Army Strategic Planning Guidance 2014*, c. 2014. As of June 9, 2015:
http://www.g8.army.mil/pdf/Army_Strategic_Planning_Guidance2014.pdf

U.S. Army Central, "RAF Assessments," Fragmentary Order 6, August 14, 2014, to "RAF Implementation," Operations Order 14-021, August 10, 2014.

U.S. Army Training and Doctrine Command, *The U.S. Army Operating Concept: Win in a Complex World—2020–2040*, U.S. Army Training and Doctrine Command Pamphlet 525-3-1, October 31, 2014. As of August 13, 2016:
http://www.tradoc.army.mil/tpubs/pams/tp525-3-1.pdf

U.S. Army Training and Doctrine Command Pamphlet 525-3-1—*See* U.S. Army Training and Doctrine Command, 2014.

U.S. Code, Title 10, Armed Forces, Subtitle A, General Military Law, Part I, Organization and General Military Powers, Chapter 6, Combatant Commands, Section 168, Military-to-Military Contacts and Comparable Activities.

U.S. Department of Defense, *National Defense Strategy*, June 2008. As of July 21, 2016:
http://www.defense.gov/Portals/1/Documents/pubs/2008NationalDefenseStrategy.pdf

———, *Sustaining U.S. Global Leadership: Priorities for 21st Century Defense*, January 2012. As of April 23, 2016:
http://archive.defense.gov/news/Defense_Strategic_Guidance.pdf

———, *Quadrennial Defense Review 2014*, March 4, 2014. As of July 21, 2016:
http://www.defense.gov/Portals/1/features/defenseReviews/QDR/
2014_Quadrennial_Defense_Review.pdf